1. KAHILI GINGER

Hedychium gardnerianum Sheppard ex Ker-Gawl

Family: Zingiberaceae (Ginger family)

Origin: Native to India, the Himalayas and adjacent regions[78]

Distribution: Introduced to Australia[16], Cook Islands, French Polynesia, Jamaica, Federated States of Micronesia, New Caledonia, New Zealand, Portugal, La Reunion Island (France), South Africa, Swaziland, United States (Kaua'i, Maui and Hawai'i Island) [31]

Ethnobotanical uses in native regions: Medicine[2], leaf used for diabetes[66], decoration in festivals[68]

The colorful flowers of *H. gardnerianum,* notice the red stamen. Photo: M.L.S

Ethnobotanical uses in non-native regions: Medicine[1], anti-microbial properties[42], potential anti-tumor treatment for cancer[37], ornamental

Pollination syndrome: Insect pollinated in Europe[18]; some sources say unknown in Hawai'i[65] but likely insect

Dispersal mechanisms: Fruit and seed-eating birds spread seeds; also spreads vegetatively by rhizomes

Invasion biology: Kāhili ginger is public enemy number one to our Hawaiian forests because of its invasion modus operandi. This plant reproduces both vegetatively via rhizomes and also sexually by seed with each flowering stalk producing on average 250 bright red seeds[12]. The color is designed to attract birds in order for it to be dispersed. This is a contributing factor that has aided kāhili ginger in spreading rapidly over large areas. The seeds seem to have extremely successful germination rates when both transported by birds and falling directly from the old flower stalk.

Rhizomes (the thick "root" part comparable to what is eaten on edible ginger) are storage organs, retaining nutrients and moisture for the plant. And although ginger grows well in soil, it is not necessarily a vital requirement for the plant's survival. Seeds that land on nurse logs, mossy nooks and branches of trees and even rocks are able to grow (largely because of the rhizomes) and, more often than

Dried flower head
Photo: M.L.S.

A thick stand of kāhili ginger (light green in center) as seen from Pihea trail. Photo: M.L.S

not, develop into mature plants which then can form a colony of its own. One study found that in Hawai'i, adult kahili ginger appears to create an advantageous environment for its own offspring as well as that of strawberry guava (*Psidium cattleianum*) [47], another weedy species on our list. Through prolific growth, kāhili ginger forms thick mats of rhizomes which leads to a significant reduction in native tree-seedlings[47] and species diversity, eventually causing the formation of a mostly monotypic stand of *Hedychium gardnerianum*. Do not confuse kāhili ginger with yellow ginger (*Hedychium flavescens*), which does not have the same fragrance or bright red stamen like the invasive one.

2. AUSTRALIAN TREE FERN (ATF)
Cyathea cooperi (Hook. ex F. Muell.) Domin
Syn: Sphaeropteris cooperi (F. Mueller) R.M. Tyron

<u>Family</u>: Cyatheaceae

<u>Origin</u>: Native to Queensland from Cooktown south and New South Wales as far south as the Illawarra district of Australia[34].

<u>Distribution</u>: Introduced in other parts of Australia (Western & Syndey), Tahiti Island, Mauritius (Africa), New Caledonia, New Zealand, Reunion Is. (France), United States (Hawaiʻi, Maui, Molokaʻi, Lānaʻi, Oʻahu and Kauaʻi Islands)[57,30,4].

<u>Ethnobotanical uses in native regions</u>: Food (the apex of the trunk containing a core of white starch was eaten raw or baked and unopened fronds were eaten raw or after roasting)[51,39]; Used in modern times as an ornamental plant.

Large *C. cooperi* with people at base for scale. Photo: KRCP

<u>Ethnobotanical uses in non-native regions</u>: Ornamental (sometimes erroneously marketed as Hawaiian *hāpuʻu*)

<u>Pollination syndrome</u>: None (not a seed-bearing plant)

<u>Dispersal mechanisms</u>: Tiny wind-born spores (smaller than a grain of sand)

<u>Invasion biology</u>: Ferns belong to a group of plants that are much older and more primitive than flowering plants on the evolutionary scale, and one of the traits associated with this ancient group is the production of spores (not seeds)- a method of plant reproduction that does not involve flowers and pollination (amongst other things). For details on this, please reference fern life cycles. *Cyathea cooperi* can hold thousands of tiny spores in each sporagia, and on each frond, hundreds of sporangia are present. All that is needed to disperse the minute spores is wind, and one ATF has the potential to produce an enormous amount of offspring.

Characteristic white scales of the Australian tree fern. Photo: M.L.S.

Typically, ferns need a moist substrate in order for germination to occur, and the upland regions of Kauaʻi have no shortage of this, which is why their establishment has been successful especially in Kōkeʻe, the Alakaʻi, and upper valleys that attach to these areas. In Hawaiʻi, it is known that wind blown ATF spores can travel over 12 km (7 miles). This was observed on Maui where parent ATF plants in Hāna nurseries spread to Kīpahulu Valley[4]. The Australian tree fern is often sold in nurseries and commonly mistaken for the native tree fern, hāpuʻu (*Cibotium* spp.). If you are looking for tree ferns to plant, make sure you do not choose the Australian tree fern (*C. cooperi*).

In its native environment, *C. cooperi* acts as as a pioneer species and is found along edges, in light gaps, road cuts and along streams[43]. In the Hawaiian Islands, Australian tree ferns are able to colonize these areas in native forests, displacing native understory species and the slower growing Hawaiian *hāpuʻu*. The trunks of Hawaiian tree ferns maintain high local species diversity because they function as germination and establishment sites for native seedlings. *C. cooperi* does not allow for dense growth of native epiphytic species and one study by Medeiros *et al.* found more than ten times as many species were growing on the trunks of native tree ferns as compared to the trunks of Australian tree ferns[43].

3. STRAWBERRY GUAVA/WAIAWI
Psidium cattleianum Sabine

Family: Myrtaceae (Myrtle family)

Origin: Native to the Atlantic coast of Brazil[63]

Distribution: Introduced to Australia, Rapa Nui (Easter Island), Comoro Islands, Cook Islands, France (La Reunion Island), French Polynesia, Fiji Islands, Himalayas (Doon Valley)[52],

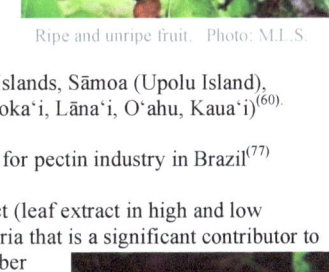

Ripe and unripe fruit. Photo: M.L.S.

Japan (Bonin Islands), Federated States of Micronesia (Pohnpei), Mauritius Islands, New Caledonia, New Zealand, Palau, Pitcairn Islands, Sāmoa (Upolu Island), Seychelles Islands, United States (Florida[23], Hawaiʻi, Maui, Molokaʻi, Lānaʻi, Oʻahu, Kauaʻi)[60].

Ethnobotanical uses in native regions: Food[20]; potential material for pectin industry in Brazil[77]

Ethnobotanical uses in non-native regions: Pharmacology prospect (leaf extract in high and low concentrations kills and suppresses *Streptococcus mutans*, a bacteria that is a significant contributor to human tooth decay)[9]; antibacterial & antifungal[15]; food and timber

Pollination syndrome: Bees and insects

Dispersal mechanisms: Feral pigs and fruit-eating birds spread seed

Invasion biology: While not an aggressive plant in its native environment[28], in Hawaiʻi and most other places it has been introduced to, strawberry guava is a vigorous invader of native plant communities. Its successful invasion can be contributed to a variety of factors. First, *Psidium cattleianum* is able to occupy and tolerate a broad range of environmental conditions, making it a hardy plant. One study in Hawaiʻi found strawberry guava in 23 different vegetation types ranging from dry grassland to tall, native forest[32]. Shade tolerance is an attribute that allows for the seeds to germinate and establish themselves in areas too dark for other plants, thus increasing the habitats *P. cattleianum* is able to occupy.

New flower. Photo: M.L.S.

Strawberry guava is fast growing and bears a substantial amount of fruit which translates to a substantial amount of seeds. Some counts from different sites on Hawaiʻi Island found guavas containing 25-70 seeds per fruit[29]. Guava relies heavily on dispersal via animals, especially feral pigs. The fruit is eaten by pigs and birds, passed through their digestive system and deposited back into the earth where seeds germinate and grow.

Camouflage bark is an easy identifier of strawberry guava. Photo: M.L.S.

Allelopathy is used by strawberry guava to maximize its potential. This is a process where the plant releases biochemicals, likely from its roots or leaves, that suppresses the germination and growth of plant species around it. Allelopathy plays a major role in assisting *P. cattleianum*'s formation of dense, monotypic (one species) stands. Lastly, strawberry guava's robust growth contributes to its persistence and difficulty to control. Cutting branches and even the entire stump just causes many new shoots to emerge, barely harming the tree.

4. CHINESE PRIVET
Ligustrum sinense Lour.

Family: Oleaceae (Olive family)

Origin: Native to China, Laos, Taiwan and Vietnam[26,35,45]

Distribution: Introduced to American Sāmoa & Western Sāmoa, Australia, Fiji, France (La Reunion Island), Guam, New Caledonia, New Zealand[59], United States (AL, AR, CT, FL, GA, HI [Hawai'i, O'ahu & Kaua'i], KY, LA, MA, MD, MO, MS, NC, NJ, OK, RI, SC, TN, TX, VA)[74]

White flowers of Chinese privet. Photo: Kay Koike

Ethnobotanical uses in native regions:
Also known as chuang xiong, it is used in Chinese medicine: The root is an anodyne, antibacterial, antifungal, antirheumatic, antispasmodic, emmenagogue, diaphoretic, hypotensive and a sedative[81, 19, 7]. Also used for menstrual disorders, post-partum bleeding, coronary heart disease, poor circulation and headaches[7] as well as for the treatment of gout[19].

Ethnobotanical uses in non-native regions: Ornamental

Pollination syndrome: Unknown, likely bees and insects[69]

Dispersal mechanisms: Fruit-eating birds spread seed[69]

Invasion biology: Privet makes an enormous amount of fruit, and is capable of producing up to one million seeds per plant[80]. It relies on birds to eat the fruit and transport its seed, which is why this plant has a large range potential. It is unknown how long the seeds can remain viable in the seed bank. Privet is a robust bush that grows quickly, forming tightly packed, impenetrable thickets. It uses this to crowd and shade out native vegetation and create habitat for other robust, weedy species that can better tolerate competition[80].

Close up of leaves. Photo: M.L.S.

L. sinense growing in a monotypic stand. Photo: Kay Koike

Many species of privet (*Ligustrum*) defend themselves against herbivory (especially from insects) by producing phenolic compounds in their leaves which inhibit digestive enzymes and proteins[36]. Another defense against herbivory may be its ability to re-sprout from root fragments. If the leafy parts of this plant was eaten or stripped off, it would not die because of the ability of the roots to re-grow. This makes privet especially difficult for humans to remove manually as the entire root mass must be pulled up.

5. SMOKEBUSH

Buddleia madagascariensis Lam.

Family: Buddleiaceae

Origin: Native to Madagascar[78]

Distribution: Introduced to Australia, Fiji, Florida, Hawai'i (Hawai'i island, Maui, O'ahu, Kaua'i), New Caledonia, New Zealand, South Africa[56,70]

B. madagascariensis invading a valley. Photo: KRCP

Ethnobotanical uses in native regions: Leaves used to treat asthma, coughs, and bronchitis[21,33]; The whole plant and seeds are used for spiritual purposes, digestive problems, and for low energy/strength[38].

Ethnobotanical uses in non-native regions: Ornamental; used to attract butterflies

Pollination syndrome: Buddleia is a genus known to attract butterflies, bees, insects and even hummingbirds, although the latter are not present in Hawai'i[8].

Powdery looking leaves and yellow flowers of smokebush. Photo: KRPC

Dispersal mechanism: Birds disperse fruit[56,] but the seeds could also be washed down hill during heavy rains and dispersed in such a way. Stems are able to grow roots and spread vegetatively[70].

Invasion biology: *Buddleia madagascarensis* is an opportunist and is one of the first species to colonize heavily disturbed areas if it is profuse in that region. This plant displays aggressive growth that enables it to crowd-out native plants (that grow slower) and form large, monotypic thickets. Purple berry-like fruits are produced and each bear numerous, tiny seeds which are appealing to, and spread by birds (thus increasing the potential range and ability to spread). *Buddleia madagascarensis* also spreads vegetatively as roots can form at the nodes on stems. This escalates its invasiveness allowing the plant an added advantage of protection from herbivory and physical damage to the branches. With this in mind, it is very important that cuttings/clippings of this plant are disposed of properly making manual removal an even more difficult process.

After fires, it is reported that Buddleia readily resprouts and will replace the old thicket that was damaged by the fire within a year[70]. Because roots are able to protect themselves from damage, this amplifies the difficulty in removing underground parts manually. On a note of caution, some people experience respiratory problems when working in close contact with this plant.

Buddleia madagascarensis takes on a vine-like habit. Pictured here, it is climbing up trees. Photo: KRCP

6. DOGTAIL BUDDLEIA
Buddleia asiatica Lour.

<u>Family</u>: Buddleiaceae

<u>Origin</u>: Native from western Pakistan and central India to southern China, Taiwan and Malesia[78]

<u>Distribution</u>: Introduced to Guam, Hawai'i (Hawai'i Island, Maui, Moloka'i, Lāna'i, O'ahu, Kaua'i), Saipan and Tinian island[55]

<u>Ethnobotanical uses in native regions</u>: Used as an abortifacient, to treat skin problems[14,44] and skin diseases[40]. Used for its wood[27], as a drink and food coloring[22], and fodder substitute[40]

<u>Ethnobotanical uses in non-native regions</u>: Ornamental, to attract butterflies

Buddleia asiatica tree. Photo: M.L.S

<u>Pollination syndrome</u>: Bees, moths and butterflies[64]

<u>Dispersal mechanism</u>: Small capsules are winged and dispersed by the wind[55,49].

<u>Invasion biology</u>: *Buddleia asiatica* can inhabit a variety of environments and is

ecologically versatile, which on its own is a dangerous situation. Compounding this is the dispersal mechanism for *B. asiatica* - wind-which has assisted its spread and establishment on the island. This species was not even recorded as present on Kaua'i until a few years ago and it has already established itself across the island with noticeable populations existing in Wainiha, Wai'alae, and Kōke'e [12].

Seeds of *B. asiatica*
Photo: M.L.S

Leaves of *B. asiatica*. Photo: M.L.S

    Buddleia asiatica invades disturbed areas such as the sides of trails[17] and road cuts and can grow in poor soil. It is robust and can tolerate drought and atmospheric pollution[64] further adding to the list of how it can out-compete native plant ecosystems. This plant can reproduce vegetatively with stem cuttings, so proper disposal of clippings is a must. It also tolerates damage to branches and foliage, as would be required of shrubs used for forage, making manual removal difficult.

B. asiatica flowers. Photo: M.L.S

7. NEW ZEALAND TEA/MANUKA
Leptospermum scoparium J.R. & G. Forster

Family: Myrtaceae (Myrtle family)

Origin: Native to New Zealand and Tasmania, Australia[78]

Distribution: Introduced to Cook Islands (Rarotonga) and Hawai'i (O'ahu, Lāna'i, Kaua'i)[78, 58]

Ethnobotanical uses in native regions: Māori use the bark as a sedative, for burns, treatment of skin diseases, colds, and as a mouthwash[50,5] A compress is made for aches and pains, and various parts of the plant are used to treat broken limbs, scabies, kidney and urinary problems, nausea and stomach pain[5].

Recently in New Zealand, it has been discovered that when honey is made with *L. scoparium*, a compound known as methylglyoxal occurs and this type of honey, known as *manukā* honey, is used to help stomach ulcers, sore throats & colds, skin ulcers, wounds, boils, minor burns, infections and MRSA (superbug) because of its antibacterial properties[41,71].

Ethnobotanical uses in non-native regions: Medicinal honey[71], ornamental

Pollination syndrome: Bees & insects

Dispersal mechanism: Wind[3]

Invasion biology: The fruit of New Zealand tea is a dry capsule much like that of the *lehua (Metrosideros polymorpha)* tree (same family). Inside are numerous seeds; small and light in order to be carried and dispersed by the wind. It has been recorded as successful in colonizing disturbed areas such as goat-eroded ridges and altered forest landscapes[78, 67]. This plant can grow as a shrub or small tree, and once established in an area, thickets form and crowd out native vegetation[67].

Like guava and many members of the Myrtaceae family, New Zealand tea demonstrates having allelopathic activity[3] (giving off biochemicals that inhibit the growth of surrounding vegetation). This may contribute to its ability to out-compete native plants.

Flowers of *manukā* (*L. scoparium*) can be white or pinkish in color. Photo: Kay Koike

8. BLACK WATTLE
Acacia mearnsii DeWild

Family: Fabaceae (Bean & pea family)

Origin: Native to New South Wales, Tasmania and Australia[78]

Distribution: Introduced to China, India, Israel, Italy, La Reunion Island, Madagascar, New Zealand, Portugal, Rapa Nui (Easter Island), Rarotonga (Cook Islands), Ryukyu islands (Japan), Seychelle islands, South Africa, Taiwan, USA (California, Hawai'i Island, Maui, Kaho'olawe, Lāna'i, Moloka'i, O'ahu and Kaua'i)[54,73,25].

Ethnobotanical uses in native regions: Some Aboriginal clans used it for medicine[13]. Australian settlers used it for framing fences and houses[24] and continue to use it for tanning leather materials[53].

Flowers and leaves of *A. mearnsii.*
Photo: M.L.S

Ethnobotanical uses in non-native regions: Agroforestry, fuel, charcoal, poles, props, green manure, windbreaks, nitrogen fixation in soil, prevention of soil erosion and tannin for leather materials[24].

Pollination syndrome: Bees and insects[53]

Dispersal mechanism: Gravity; seeds are also potentially moved by rodents or birds[11]

Invasion biology: Although some publications state that black wattle does not seem to actively disperse itself[25] for example, by using wind, it has managed to establish itself over quite a range. Allelopathic chemicals in its leaves and branches can be poisonous to even its own young seedlings[12]. One

important aspect contributing to the invasive nature of black wattle is the prolific amount of long-lived seeds produced that stay in the seed bank[25]. Germination of these seeds are potentially triggered by fire which would kill off other vegetation and give only black wattle a chance to grow. Many new shoots emerge from the base of trees after fire adding to the robustness of this species[54].

A thick stand of black wattle along Kumuwela road.
Photo: M.L.S

One of the agroforestry uses of black wattle is to prevent soil erosion. While native vegetation & ecosystems are much more efficient at erosion prevention, black wattle in Hawai'i may mitigate erosion only at the cost to the watershed. Because *A. mearnsii* can reach great heights, a large canopy and biomass intercepts rainfall (part of the soil-erosion mitigation) leaving less water for surrounding plants. Some studies have demonstrated through decreased streamflow that black wattle has high rates of water up-take and transpiration (how plants release water as a vapor through leaves etc...)[25]. These processes steal water away from native plants and the watershed.

9. PALM GRASS
Setaria palmifolia (J. Konig) Stapf

<u>Family</u>: Poaceae (Grass family)

<u>Origin</u>: Native to China, Taiwan, Japan, India, Nepal, Pakistan, Sri Lanka, Myanmar, Thailand, Indonesia, Malaysia, Papua New Guinea, Phillipines[75]

<u>Distribution</u>: Introduced to Australia, Cook Islands, Fiji, French Polynesia (Tahiti), Hawai'i (Hawai'i, Maui, Moloka'i, Lāna'i, O'ahu, Kaua'i), New Caledonia, New Zealand, Rapa Nui, Sāmoa, Solomon Islands[62]

Palmgrass growing on a stream bank amongst other weedy species. Its leaves look like the first leaves of palms. Photo: M.L.S.

<u>Ethnobotanical uses in native regions</u>: Used as medicine in Taiwan[72]; in Papua New Guinea used medicinally[46], ceremonially[76] and stems & young leaves are eaten; in Malaysia mixture given for irregular menses[10], used to treat skin disorders in Philippines[6]

<u>Ethnobotanical uses in non-native regions</u>: Ornamental

<u>Pollination syndrome</u>: Assumed to be wind pollinated (as most grasses are).

<u>Dispersal mechanism</u>: Wind or granivorous birds[62] disperse seed; also spreads vegetatively with rhizomes

<u>Invasion biology</u>: Palm grass can grow up to 2 meters in height and is effective at shading out herbaceous plants. Like many grass species, it is an effective colonizer of disturbed areas and openings in the forest. It can also be found growing along streams.

Because it seeks out areas which are more open, it is hardy and can live in a range of environments from full sun to moderate shade, hot and cool climates, and tolerates wind, salt, drought, occasional submersion, and frost[79]. With strong rhizomes, plants crowd out other vegetation and form dense, monotypic stands. These thickets also prevent seedlings from other species from establishing.

Palmgrass is well adapted to fire[67] and rhizomes and root masses are able to readily re-sprout after damage making removal difficult. It also protects itself with fiberglass-like hairs.

Close-up of parallel veination on palmgrass leaf blades. Photo: M.L.S

10. SAWTOOTH/PRICKLY FLORIDA BLACKBERRY
Rubus argutus Link

Family: Rosaceae (Rose family)

Origin: Native to central and eastern United States[78]

Distribution: Introduced to Hawai'i (Hawai'i island, Maui, Moloka'i, O'ahu, Kaua'i) and New Zealand[61]

Flowers of *Rubus argutus*. Photo: M.L.S

Ethnobotanical uses in native regions: Used by Cherokee as a stimulant, catharitic, throat and oral aid, tonic, urinary aid, venereal aid, food/fruit, anti-diarrheal, anti-rheumatic (internal), dermatological and hemorrhoid aid for piles[48]; used by non-Cherokee for food such as preserves and jellies.

Ethnobotanical uses in non-native regions: Food

Pollination syndrome: Bees and insects

Dispersal mechanism: Frugivorous (fruit-eating) birds are the main means by which blackberry is dispersed.

Invasion biology: Blackberry, like most plants on this list, is a colonizer of disturbed areas. Disturbed forest floor and/or canopy has been found to encourage the growth and development of blackberry seedlings. Once established, blackberry forms thick and thorny brambles.

This plant also spreads vegetatively, as stems touching the ground are sometimes able to sprout roots, further expanding the tangle of thorns[67].

Sharp thorns line the branches and leaf midribs. Photo: M.L.S

Ripe blackberry fruit. Photo: M.L.S

Even when a stem or branch dies and dries up, the thorns and bramble persists for a long time, making the thicket just as difficult for other vegetation to grow.

Each mature blackberry produces many fruit that are attractive to birds that eat the fruit and drop the seeds. Blackberry is tolerant of mild shade and fire[67], allowing for surface branches to be cut or damaged while underground roots readily re-sprout.

Thorny brambles colonize disturbed areas. Photo: M.L.S

LITERATURE CITED:

1. Abraham, Z., D.S. Bhakuri, H.S. Garg, B.N. Mehrola, and G.K Patnaik. 1986. Screening of Indian plants for biological activity. Part XII. Indian J. Exp. Biol. 24: 48-68.
2. Ahmed, Ayesha Ashraf and S.K. Borthakur. 2005. Ethnobotanical wisdom of Khasis (Hyn\~niew Treps) of Meghalaya. India. Rs. 1250.00. ISBN 81-211-0434-3. Available via: http://indianmedicine.eldoc.ub.rug.nl/root/A2/164a/ <June 2010>.
3. Alien Plants of Hawai'i, UH Botany. Leptospermum scoparium. http://www.botany.hawaii.edu/faculty/cw_smith/lep_sco.htm <July 2010>.
4. Australian tree fern (Cyathea cooperi). 2008. Hawai'i Invasive Species Partnership. http://www.hawaiiinvasivespecies.org/pests/australiantreefern.html <June 2010>.
5. Best Practice. May 2008. Demystifying Rongoā Māori: Traditional Māori Healing. Issue 13. Pp. 32-36. http://www.bpac.org.nz/magazine/2008/may/rongoa.asp <July 2010>.
6. Bodner, C. C. and R. E. Gereau. 1988. A Contribution to Bontoc Ethnobotany. Economic Botany 42(3):307-369.
7. Bown. D. 1995. Encyclopaedia of Herbs and their Uses. Dorling Kindersley, London. ISBN 0-7513-020-31
8. Brickell, C. and J. D. Zuk. 1997. The American Horticultural Society A-Z Encyclopedia of Garden Plants. DK Publishing, Inc., NY.
9. Brighenti, F.L., S.B.I Luppens, A.C.B Delbem, D.M. Deng, M.A. Hoogenkamp, E. Gaetti-Jardim, H.L. Dekker, W. Crielaard, and J.M. ten Cate. 2008. Effect of Psidium cattleianum leaf extract on Streptococcus mutans viability, protien expression and acid production. Caries Research 48:148-154.45.
10. Burkill, I. 1966. A Dictionary of the Economic Products of the Malay Peninsula., 2nd ed. Ministry of Agriculture and Co-Operatives, Kuala Lumpur, Malaysia.
11. Carr, G.D. Acacia mearnsii University of Hawaii, Botany Department. http://www.botany.hawaii.edu/faculty/carr/aca_mea.htm <July 2010>.
12. Cassel, Katie. Personal communication. 2010.
13. CERES (Center for Education & Research in Environmental Strategies). 2010. Bushfood catalogue. http://www.ceres.org.au/bushfoodcatalogue <July 2010>.
14. Chopra. R. N., Nayar. S. L. and Chopra. I. C. 1986. Glossary of Indian Medicinal Plants (Including the Supplement). Council of Scientific and Industrial Research, New Delhi.
15. Cochrane, C.B. 1999. Antibacterial and antifungal screening of Florida's exotic invasive plant species. In D.T. Jones and B.W. Gamble, editors. Proceedings of the 1998 joint symposium of the Florida Exotic Pest Plant Council and the Florida Native Plant Society. South Florida Water Management District, West Palm Beach, Florida. Pp.205-216.
16. Csurhes, S. and Hannan-Jones, M. 2008. Pest plant risk assessment: Kahili ginger (Hedychium gardnerianum), White ginger (Hedychium coronarium), Yellow ginger (Hedychium flavescens). Biosecurity Queensland Department of Primary Industries and Fisheries. August 2008.
17. Daehler, C. U. of Hawai'i at Mānoa: Botany Department. www.botany.hawaii.edu/faculty/daehler/wra/full/Buddleja_asiatica_SMJ.xls <July 2010>. Cited in Aluka Inc. African Species Plant Checklist Webpage. [Accessed 2008] http://www.aluka.org/action/doBrowse?sa=1&sa=1&br=tax-epithets-derived%7Cnamed-as%7Cplant-name-family

18. D.A.I.S.I.E. Species Factsheet: Hedychium gardnerianum. http://www.europe-aliens.org/speciesFactsheet.do?speciesId=5464# <June 2010>.
19. Duke. J. A. and Ayensu. E. S. 1985. Medicinal Plants of China. Reference Publications, Inc. ISBN 0-917256-20-4
20. Eichemberg, M.T., M.C. de Mello Amorozo, and L. Cunha de Moura. 2009. Species composition and plant use in old urban homegardens in Rio Claro, Southeast of Brazil. Acta Botanica Brasilica 23:4. available via: http://www.scielo.br/scielo.php?pid=S0102-33062009000400016&script=sci_arttext <June 2010>.
21. Emam, A.C., A.M. Moussa, R. Faure, R. Elias, G. Balansard. 1998. Isolation of mimengoside B, a triterpenoid saponin from Buddleja madagascariensis. Journal of Ethnopharmacology. 58:3 pp.215-217.
22. Facciola. S. 1990. Cornucopia - A Source Book of Edible Plants. Kampong Publications Forest Research Institute Press. ISBN 0-9628087-0-9
23. Florida Exotic Pest Plant Council (FLEPPC). Psidium cattleianum Sabine. www.fleppc.org/ID_book/psidium%20cattleianum.pdf <June 2010>.
24. Forest, Farm, and Community Tree Network (FACT Net): NFTA 85-02. 1985. Acacia mearnsii: mutipurpose highland legume tree. http://www.winrock.org/fnrm/factnet/factpub/FACTSH/A_mearnsii.html <July 2010>.
25. Global Invasive Species Database. Ecology of Acacia mearnsii. April 2006. http://www.issg.org/database/species/ecology.asp?si=51&fr=1&sts=sss&lang=EN <July 2010>.
26. Green, P.S. 1995. Taxonomic notes relating to Ligustrum (Oleaceae). Kew Bull 50:379-386.
27. Gupta, B. L. (1928). Forest Flora of Chakrata Dehra Dun and Saharanpur Forest Division. United Provinces, Calcutta.
28. Hodges, C. S. 1988. Preliminary exploration for potential biological control agents for Psidium cattleianum . Tech. Report 66. Coop. Natl. Park Resour. Studies Unit. Univ. of Hawaii, Honolulu. 32 pp.
29. Huenneke, L.F. and P. M. Vitousek. 1989. Seedling and clonal recruitment of the invasive tree Psidium cattleianum : implications for management of native Hawaiian forests. Biological Conservation 53: 199-211.
30. Invasive Species Specialist Group (ISSG) Database: Distribution of Cyathea cooperi. http://www.invasivespecies.net/database/species/distribution.asp?si=1183&fr=1&sts=sss&lang=EN <June 2010>.
31. Invasive Species Specialist Group (ISSG) Database: Distribution of Hedychium gardnerianum. Global Invasive Species Database. http://www.issg.org/database/species/distribution.asp?si=57&fr=1&sts=&lang=EN <June 2010>.
32. Jacobi, J. D., and F. R. Warshauer. In press. The current and potential distribution of six introduced plants species in upland habitats on the island of Hawaii. In C. P. Stone, C. W. Smith, and J. T. Tunison (eds.), Alien Plant Invasions in Native Ecosystems of Hawaii: Management and Research. Univ. Hawaii Coop. Natl. Park Resour. Studies Unit. Univ. Hawaii Press, Honolulu.
33. Johnson, T. 1998. CRC ethnobotany desk reference. CRC Press LLC. Boca Raton, FL.
34. Jones, D. L. and S.C. Clemesha. 1976. Australian ferns and fern allies with notes on their cultivation. Reed, Sydney.

35. Kiew, R. 1978. Florae Malesianae praecursores. LVII. The Oleaceae of Malesia. I. The genus Ligustrum. Blumea 24:143-149.
36. Konno, K.; H. Yasui; C. Hirayama; H. Shinbo. 1998. Glycine protects against strong protein denaturing activity of oleuropein, a phenolic compound in privet leaves. Journal of Chemical Ecology. 24(4): 735-751.
37. Kumrit, I., A. Suksamrarn, P., Meepawpan, S. Songsri, and N. Nuntawong. 2009. Labdane-type diterpenes from Hedychium gardnarianum potent cytotoxicity against human small cell lung cancer cells. Phytotherapy Research, 24:7; pp. 1099-1573.
38. Lehman, A.D. 2009. Assessing ethnobotanical knowledge and resources to develop a sustainable management plan for the Lokaro reserve in southeast, Madagascar. Thesis for partial fulfillment for the degree of Master of Science in Resource Conservation, International Conservation and Development. The University of Montana: Missoula, MT. Available via: etd.lib.umt.edu/theses/available/etd.../Lehman_Ashley_thesis_final.pdf <July 2010>.
39. Low, Tim, 1991. Wild Food Plants of Australia. Mace M, Turrawan Centre via: Mary Cairncross Scenic Reserve. Rainforest bush tucker guide: http://www.mary-cairncross.com.au/rainforest-bushtucker-guide.php <June 2010>.
40. Manandhar. N. P. and S. Mananadahar. 2002. Plants and People of Nepal. Timber Press, Oregon. ISBN 0-88192-527-6
41. Mavric, E., S. Wittmann, G. Barth, and T. Henle. 2008. Identification and quantification of methylglyoxal as the dominant antibacterial constituent of Manuka (Leptospermum scoparium) honeys from New Zealand. Molecular Nutrition and Food Research 52:4. Pp.483-489.
42. Medeiros et al. 2003. Composition and antimicrobial activity of the essential oils from invasive species of the Azores, Hedychium gardnerianum and Pittosporum undulatum. Phytochemistry 64(2003) 561-565.
43. Medeiros, A.C., L.L. Loope, T. Flynn, S.J. Anderson, L.W. Cuddihy, and K.A. Wilson. 1992. Notes on the status of an invasive Australian tree fern (Cyathea cooperi) in Hawaiian rain forests. American Fern Journal 82:1 pp.27-33.
44. Medicinal Plants of Nepal Dept. of Medicinal Plants. Nepal. 1993
45. Mei-chen, C., Q. Lian-quing, P.S. Green. 1996. Oleaceae. Pages 272-320 in Z-Y Wu, P.H. Raven, eds. Flora of China. Vol. 15. Myrsinaceae to Loganicaae. Science, Beijing; Missouri Botanical Garden, St. Louis.
46. Milliken, W. (1999). Ethnobotany of the Yali of West Papua. Royal Botanic Garden Edinburgh electronic publication. Available via: rbg-web2.rbge.org.uk/ethnobotany/Yali.pdf <July 2010>.
47. Minden, V., K.J. Hennenberg, S. Porembski, and H.J. Boehmer. 2009. Invasion and management of alien Hedychium gardnerianum (kahili ginger, Zingiberaceae) alter plant species composition of a montane rainforest on the island of Hawai'i. Plant Ecology 206:2 pp.321-333.
48. Moerman, D.E. 2009. Native American Medicinal Plants: An ethnobotanical dictionary. Timber Press Inc, Oregon. ISBN 978-1-60469-053-4.
49. Motooka, P., L. Castro, D. Nelson, G. Nagai, and L. Ching. 2003. Weeds of Hawaii's Pastures and Natural Areas; An Identification and Management Guide. College of Tropical Agriculture and Human Resources, University of Hawaii at Manoa.

50. Museum of New Zealand: Te Papa Tongarewa. Manuka. http://www.tepapa.govt.nz/Education/OnlineResources/Matariki/MaoriMedicine/Pages/Manuka.aspx <July 2010>.

51. Nash, D. and Australian National Botanic Gardens. 2004. Aboriginal plant use in south eastern Austraila. Education Services. www.anbg.gov.au/education/programs/plantuse.pdf <June 2010>.

52. Negi, P.S. and P.K. Hajra. 2007. Alien flora of Doon Valley, Northwest Himalaya. Curr Sci 92:968–978. Available via: www.ias.ac.in/currsci/apr102007/968.pdf <June 2010>.

53. Nuttal, L., M. Butler, C. Gartlan and A. Ovington. 2006. Acacia mearnsii, black wattle. Corangamite Region Guidelines: Corangamite Seed Supply & Revegetation Network. http://www.ccma.vic.gov.au/GLOBAL/uploaded/Speciesnotes-Acaciamearnsii.pdf <July 2010>.

54. Pacific Island Ecosystems at Risk (PIER). Apr. 2009. Acacia mearnsii (PIER species info). http://www.hear.org/pier/species/acacia_mearnsii.htm <July 2010>.

55. Pacific Island Ecosystems at Risk (PIER). Nov. 2008. Buddleia asiatica (PIER species info). http://www.hear.org/Pier/species/buddleja_asiatica.htm <July 2010>.

56. Pacific Island Ecosystems at Risk (PIER). Jul 2008. Buddleja madagascarensis (PIER species info). http://www.hear.org/pier/species/buddleja_madagascariensis.htm <July 2010>.

57. Pacific Island Ecosystems at Risk (PIER). Jan 2008. Cyathea cooperi (PIER species info). http://www.hear.org/pier/species/cyathea_cooperi.htm <June 2010>.

58. Pacific Island Ecosystems at Risk (PIER). Dec. 2007. Leptospermum scoparium (PIER species info). http://www.hear.org/pier/species/leptospermum_scoparium.htm <July 2010>.

59. Pacific Island Ecosystems at Risk (PIER). Jan 2010. Ligustrum sinense (PIER species info). http://www.hear.org/pier/species/ligustrum_sinense.htm <June 2010>.

60. Pacific Island Ecosystems at Risk (PIER). Jan 2010. Psidium cattleianum (PIER species info). http://www.hear.org/pier/species/psidium_cattleianum.htm <June 2010>.

61. Pacific Island Ecosystems at Risk (PIER). Jan 2010. Rubus argutus (PIER species info). http://www.hear.org/pier/species/rubus_argutus.htm <July 2010>.

62. Pacific Island Ecosystems at Risk (PIER). Jan. 2010. Setaria palmifolia (PIER species info). http://www.hear.org/pier/species/setaria_palmifolia.htm <July 2010>.

63. Plant Conservation Alliance's Alien Plant Working Group. 2009. Strawberry guava (Psidium cattleianum). http://www.nps.gov/plants/alien/fact/psca1.htm <June 2010>.

64. Plants For A Future. Buddleia asiatica- plants for a future database report. http://www.pfaf.org/database/plants.php?Buddleia+asiatica <July 2010>.

65. Research needs of the of Nature Conservancy of Hawai'i. http://www.hawaii.edu/eecb/ProgInfoMinis/NCH.html <June 2010>

66. Simmonds, M.S.J. and M.J.R. Howes. 2006. Plants used in the treatment of diabetes. Taylor & Fransics Group, LLC. Traditional Medicines for Modern Times: Antidiabetic Plants pp.19-82. http://www.crcnetbase.com/doi/abs/10.1201/9781420019001.ch2 <June 2010>.

67. Smith, C.W. 1985. Impact of alien plants on Hawaii's native biota. pp. 180-250 In C.P. Stone and J.M. Scott (eds.). Hawaii's Terrestrial Ecosystems: Preservation and Management. Univ. Hawaii Coop. Natl. Resour. Studies Unit.

68. Srivastava RC and Nyishi Community. Traditional knowledge of Nyishi (Daffla) tribe of Arunchal Pradesh. Indian Journal of Traditional Knowledge Vol. 9(1), January 2010, pp.26-37.

69. Starr, F. 2003. Ligustrum spp. Pacific Island Ecosystems at Risk (PIER). www.hear.org/Pier/pdf/pohreports/ligustrum_spp.pdf <June 2010>.

70. Starr, F., K. Starr, and L. Loope. 2003. Buddleia madagascarensis. United States Geological Survey- Biological Resources Divison. Available via: www.hear.org/Pier/pdf/pohreports/buddleia_madagascariensis.pdf <July 2010>.

71. SummerGlow Apiaries Ltd. Manuka honey helps heal a range of conditions. 2003. http://manukahoney.com/resources/conditions/index.html <July 2010>.

72. Taiwan's Traditional Knowledge Website (Indigenous Knowledge, Formosa). 2003. National Taiwan University, Seed Lab. Dept. of Agronomy. http://tk.agron.ntu.edu.tw/ethnobot/DBdescr.htm <July 2010>.

73. USDA, NRCS. 2010. The PLANTS Database. National Plant Data Center, Baton Rouge, LA 70874-4490 USA. PLANTS profile for Acacia mearnsii (black wattle). http://plants.usda.gov/java/profile?symbol=ACME80 <July 2010>.

74. USDA, NRCS. 2010. The PLANTS Database. National Plant Data Center, Baton Rouge, LA 70874-4490 USA. PLANTS profile for Ligustrum sinense (Chinese privet). http://plants.usda.gov/java/profile?symbol=LISI <June 2010>.

75. USDA, ARS, National Genetic Resources Program. Germplasm Resources Information Network - (GRIN) [Online Database]. National Germplasm Resources Laboratory, Beltsville, Maryland. http://www.ars-grin.gov/cgi-bin/npgs/html/taxon.pl?33832 <July 2010>.

76. von Reis, S. and F. J. Lipp, Jr. 1982. New Plant Sources for Drugs and Foods from the New York Botanical Garden Herbarium. Harvard University Press, Cambridge MA.

77. Vriesmann, L.C., C.L.O. Petkowicz, P.I.B. Carneiro, M.E. Costa, and E. Beleski-Carneiro. 2009. Acidic polysaccharides from Psidium catteianum (Araca). Brazilian Archives of Biology and Technology 52:2 pp. 259-264. Available via: www.scielo.br/pdf/babt/v52n2/01.pdf <June 2010>.

78. Wagner, W.L., D.R. Herbst, and S.H. Sohmer. 1999. Manual of the flowering plants of Hawai'i, revised ed. Univ. Hawai'i Press and Bishop Museum Press, Honolulu. 2 vol.

79. Weedbusters. Weed information: Setaria palmifolia. http://weedbusters.co.nz/weed_info/detail.asp?WeedID=32 <July 2010>.

80. Weeds of Blue Mountains Bushland. Privet- small-leaf. http://www.weedsbluemountains.org.au/privet_small-leaf.asp <July 2010>.

81. Yeung. Him-Che. 1985. Handbook of Chinese Herbs and Formulas. Institute of Chinese Medicine, Los Angeles. ISBN 0-963971-52-2

RESEARCHED BY M. L. SPERRY
FOR
KŌKEʻE RESOURCE CONSERVATION PROGRAM

I MAU AI KA NAHELE ʻŌIWI

www.ingramcontent.com/pod-product-compliance
Lightning Source LLC
Chambersburg PA
CBHW040318010626
45792CB00023B/1014